Color, Cut & Fold

WILD ANIMALS

PRACTICE SCISSOR SKILLS!

Let's get started!

All you need is a pair of scissors, a glue stick, and markers, colored pencils, or crayons! There are stickers to add to your creations when you have finished.

①

Carefully pull out the page you want along the perforation.

②

Color both sides of the page with markers, pencils, or crayons.

③

Start at the dot.

Starting at the dot, cut out the picture around the dashed line.

Cut around dashed lines.

Glue here

Fold along dotted lines.

Where to cut?
- - - - - - - - - -
Cut along dashed lines like this.

Where to fold?
· · · · · · · · · · · · · · · · · · ·
Fold along dotted lines like this.

Where to glue?
Some of the animals should be folded and glued. Follow the instructions on each page.

Lion

You can hear a lion's roar almost five miles away.

1. Color the front and back of the lion.

3. Glue the triangle section under the flap on the left.

Glue here

2. Start cutting at the dot.

4. When you have
   finished, add
   some stickers.

Tiger

Tigers are the biggest in the cat family. They can grow to over 11 feet long!

1. Color the front and back of the tiger.

2. Start cutting at the dot.

3. Fold the line on the middle of the head, and glue the two triangles together.

Monkey

Monkeys can use their
tails to hang upside down!

2. Start cutting
at the dot.

1. Color the front and
back of the monkey.

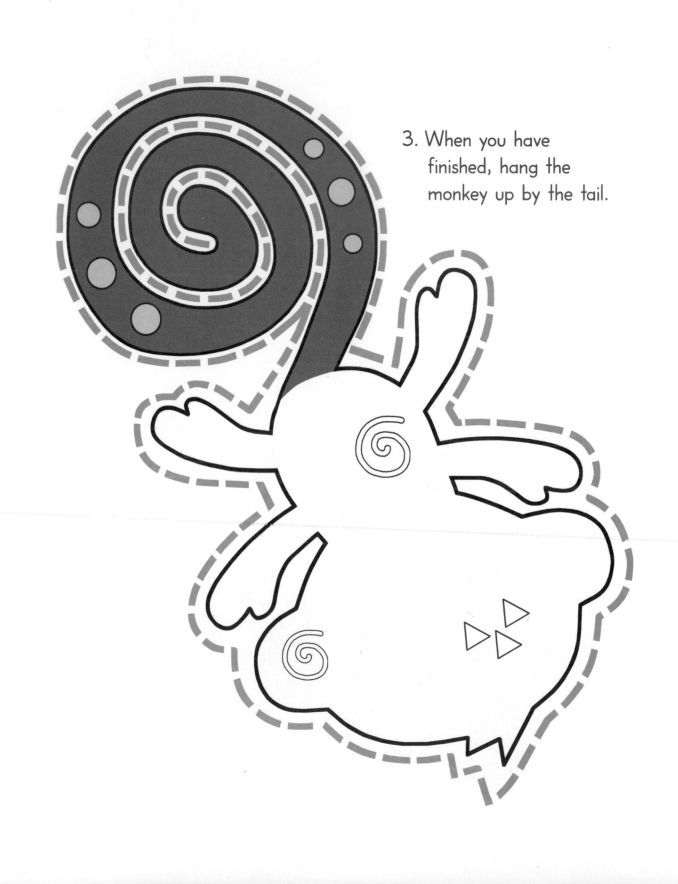

3. When you have finished, hang the monkey up by the tail.

Giraffe

Giraffes only sleep for up to 30 minutes each day!

1. Color the front and back of the giraffe.

2. Start cutting at the dot.

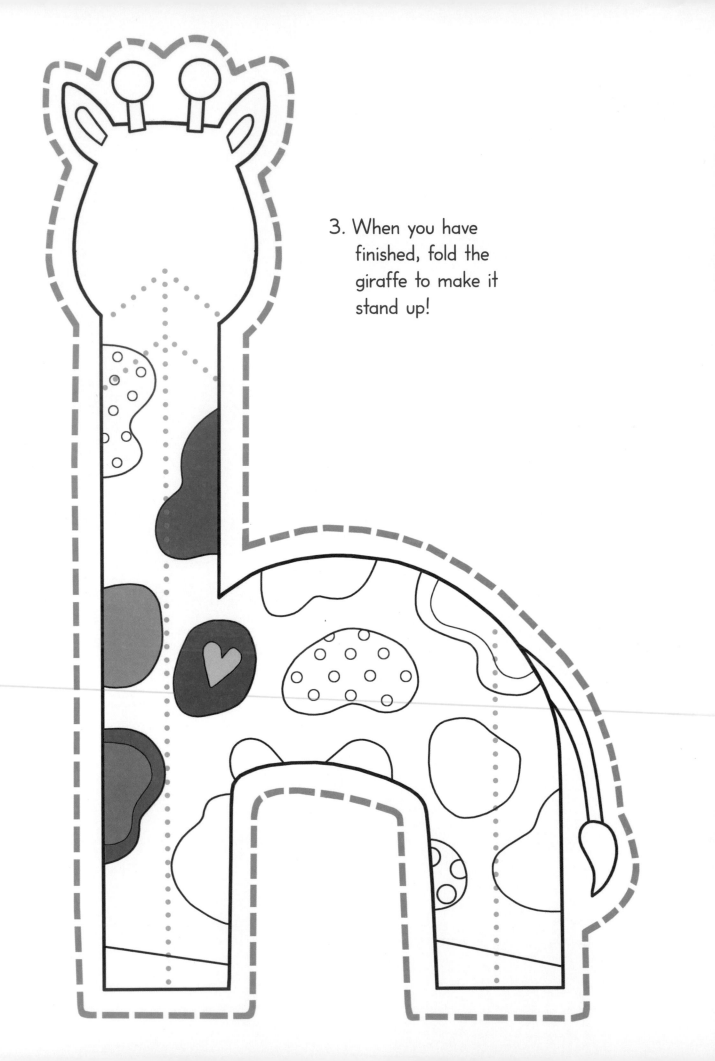

3. When you have finished, fold the giraffe to make it stand up!

Hippo

Hippo is short for hippopotamus, which means "river horse."

1. Color the front and back of the hippo.

2. Start cutting at the dot.

3. Fold in half to make
   your hippo stand up.

Crocodile

1. Color the front and back of the crocodile.

2. Start cutting at the dot.

All 13 types of crocodiles like warm, tropical weather.

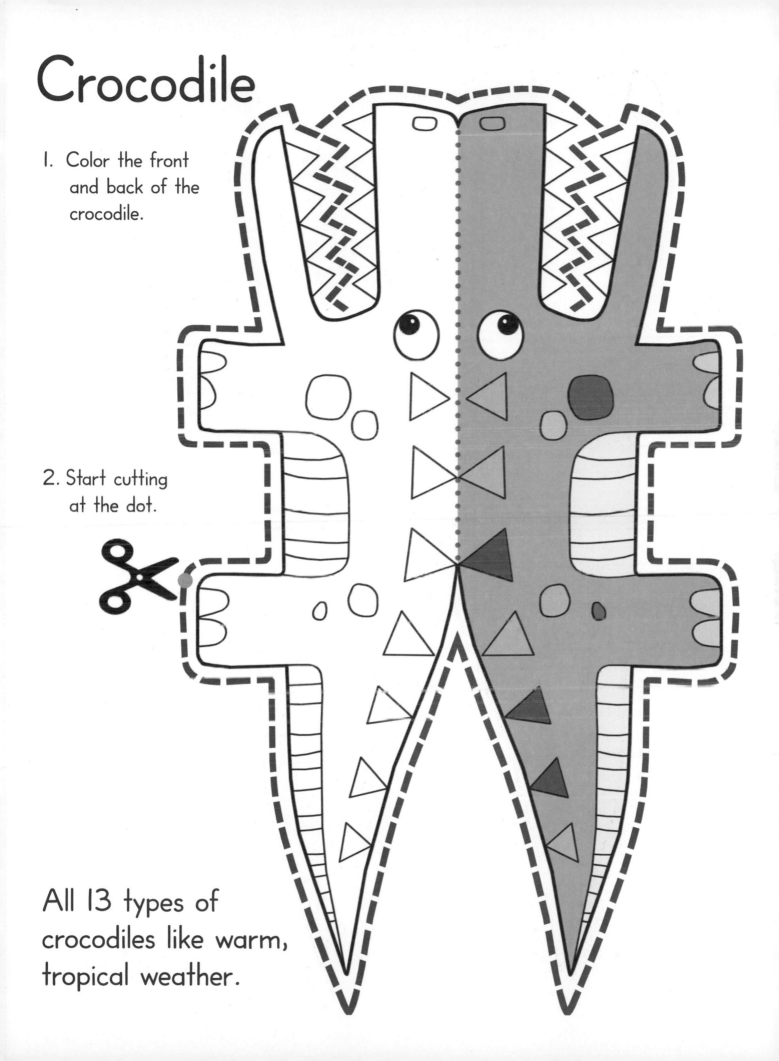

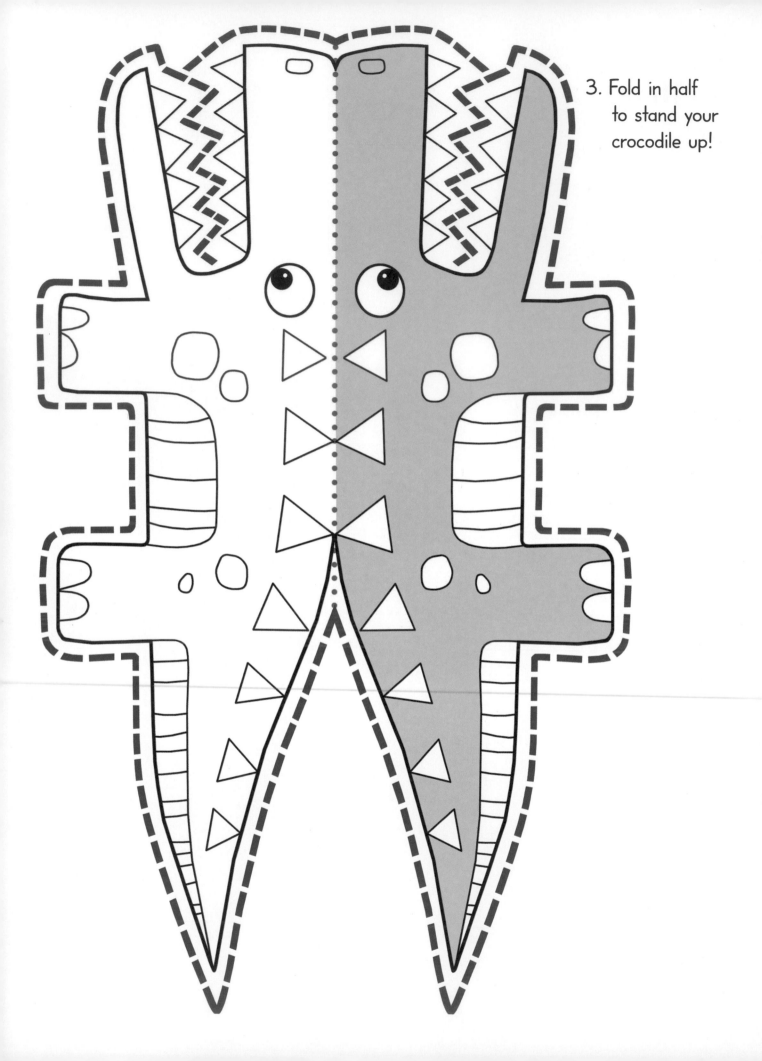

3. Fold in half to stand your crocodile up!

Rhino

Rhino is short
for rhinoceros,
which means
"nose horn."

1. Color the
   front and
   back of
   the rhino.

2. Start cutting
   at the dot.

Glue

3. Stick the triangle
   section under the
   flap with glue.

4. When you have finished, bend the legs a little to stand your rhino up.

Anteater

1. Color the front and back of the anteater.

2. Start cutting at the dot.

Anteaters use their long, sticky tongues to eat ants.

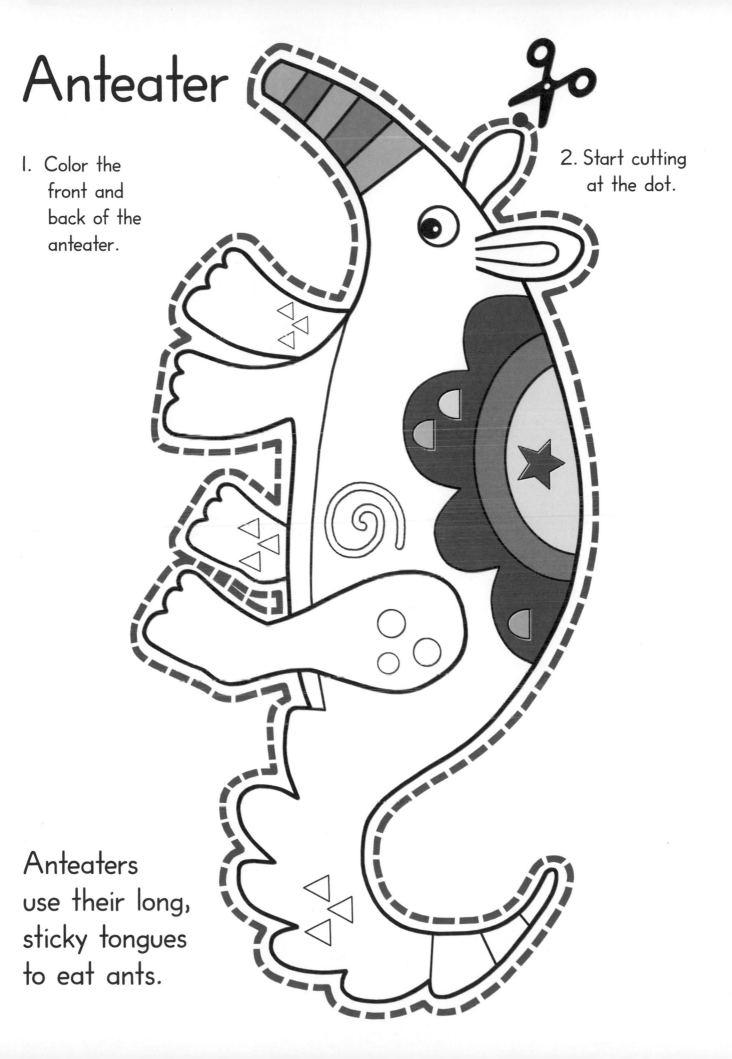

3. When you have finished, you can glue your anteater to a notebook!

Elephant

Elephants are the largest living land mammal.

1. Color the front and back of the elephant.

2. Start cutting at the dot.

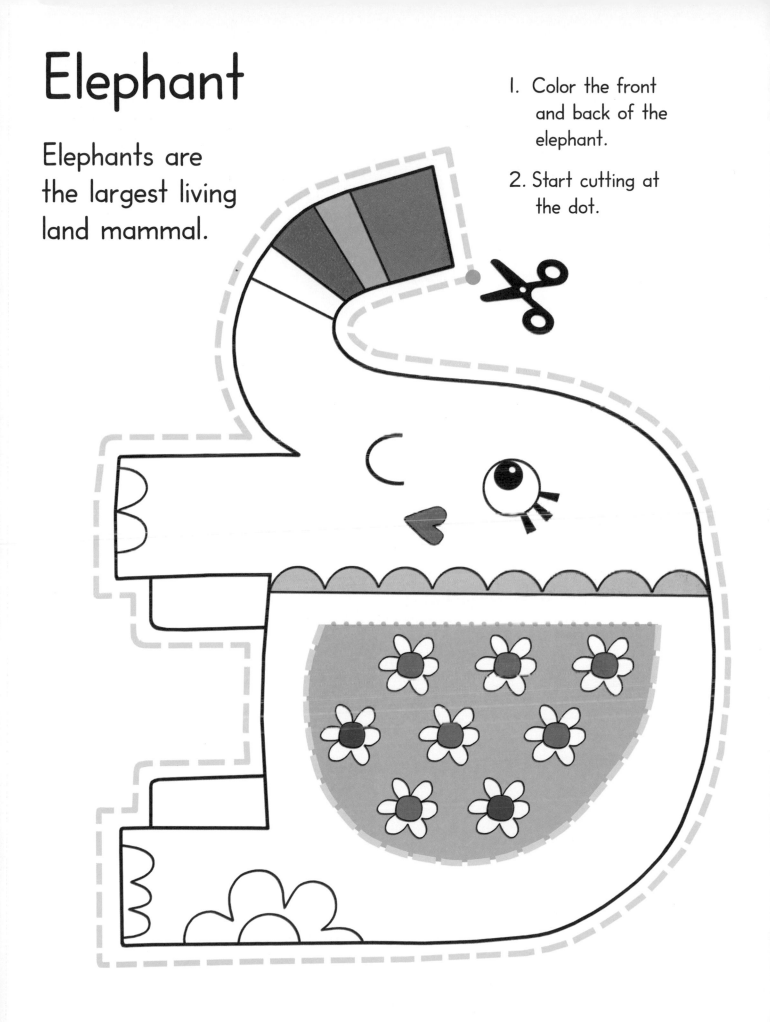

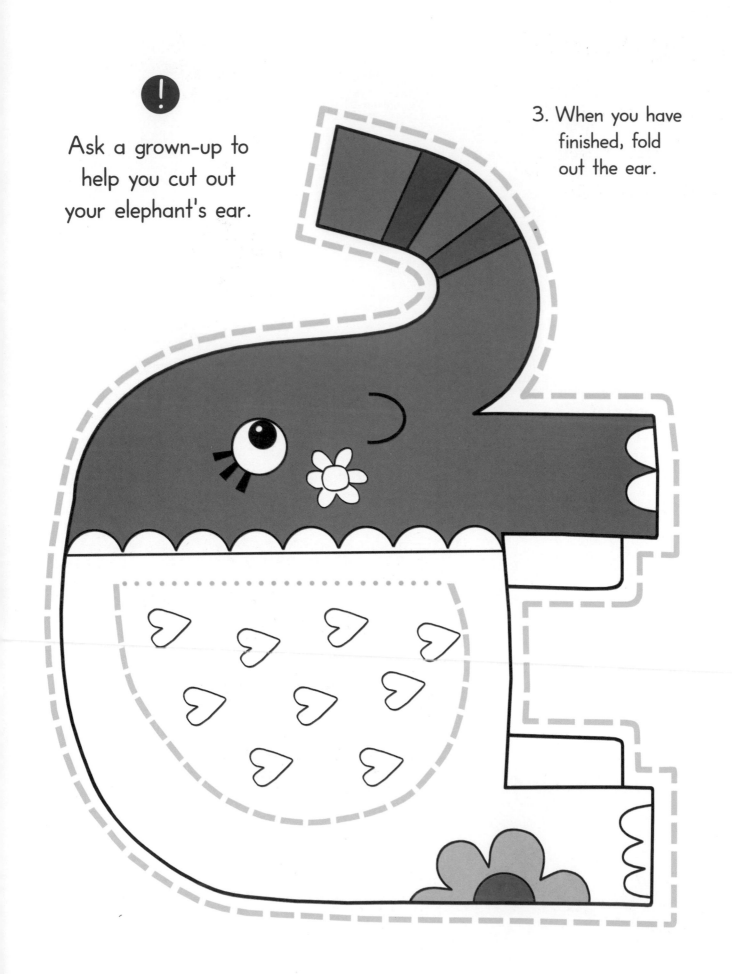

Ask a grown-up to help you cut out your elephant's ear.

3. When you have finished, fold out the ear.

Zebra

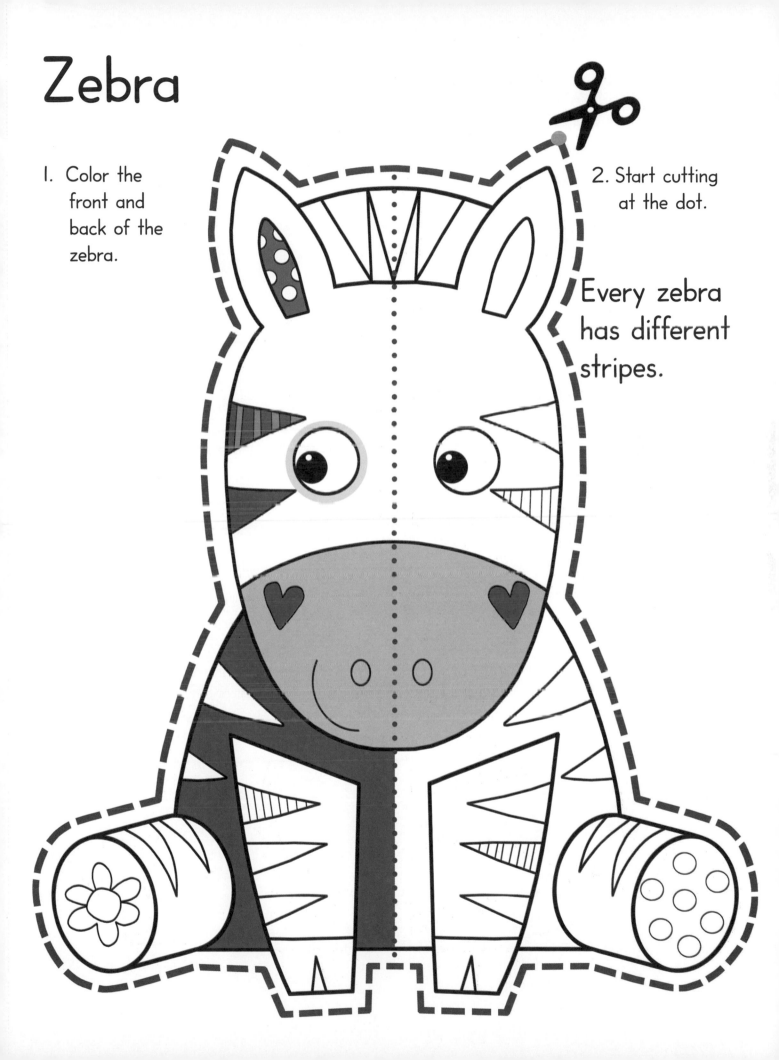

1. Color the front and back of the zebra.

2. Start cutting at the dot.

Every zebra has different stripes.

3. When you have finished, fold in half
   and unfold a little so your zebra stands.

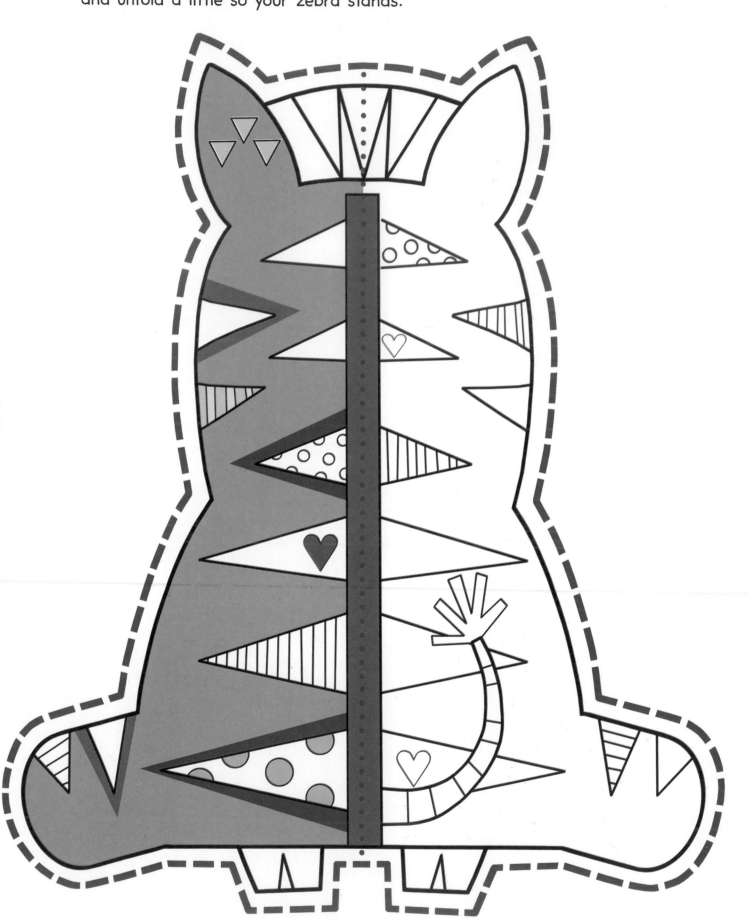

Leopard

1. Color the front and back of the leopard.

Leopards can jump almost 20 feet!

2. Start cutting at the dot.

3. Add some more spots!

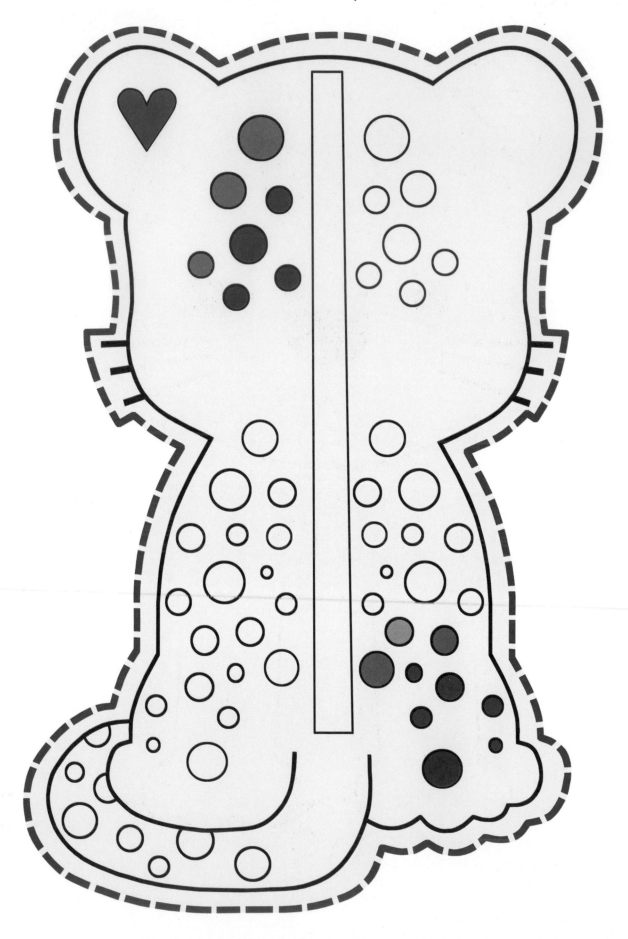

Bear

Bears can see in color, unlike most other mammals.

1. Color the front and back of the bear.

2. Start cutting at the dot.

Glue

Glue

3. For each ear, stick the section marked "Glue" to the back of the flap next to it.

4. When you have finished,
stick your bear to the
fridge as a decoration.

Sloth

Sloths live in the rainforests of
Central and South America.

1. Color the front and back
   of the sloth.

2. Start cutting at the dot.

3. Attach a piece of string to
   each end of the branch to
   hang your sloth up.

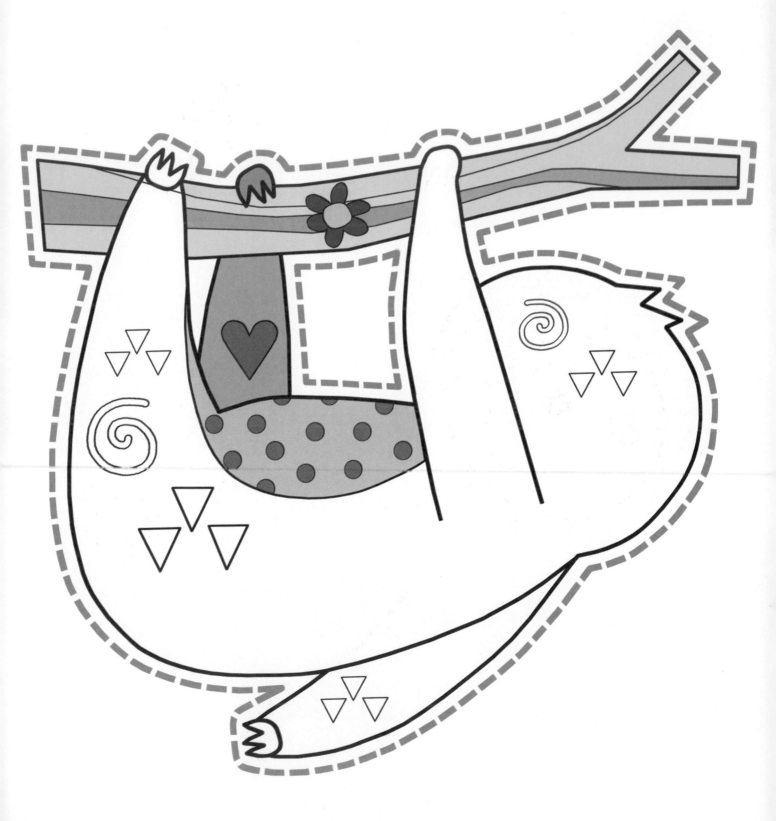

Meerkat

2. Start cutting at the dot.

1. Color the front and back of the meerkat.

!

Ask a grown-up to help cut out the meerkat's tail.

Meerkats make burrows to keep cool from the sun.

3. Draw your
   own pattern!

Toucan

Toucans are related to woodpeckers and can use their beaks like a knife.

1. Color the front and back of the toucan.

2. Start cutting at the dot.

3. When you have finished,
   you can stick your
   toucan to a door.